WHAT'S YOUR EXCUSE?

How I used my prison experience to save $100,000.

Text Copyright © 2022 by Larry Turnley

Cover art and interior illustration Copyright © 2022 by Rafiqshah

Published By: Brittany Nicole Publications

ISBN- 978-0-578-37394-2

Author: Larry L.T Turnley

Websites: www.ltlarryturnley.com

Facebook: Larry Turnley

I.G. @TurnleyLarry

PRINTED IN THE UNITED STATES OF AMERICA

DEDICATION

I dedicate this Book to Mrs.Dariel Blackledge-Washington, my former Federal Probation officer. My supporter and friend. I thank Mrs. Washington for believing in my rehabilitation efforts and for recognizing the need to create bigger roles for returning citizens in the United States Federal Probation Office. Hopefully Mrs. Washington's vision to allow returning citizens to become Federal Probation officers come to fruition one day.

Rest in Power

TABLE OF CONTENTS

FOREWORD

Dariel Blackledge-Washington
My former U.S. Probation Officer

"Life You are hereby sentenced to life in the custody of BOP." Imagine the hollowing echo of those words in one's ears. The piercing effect of those words to a man's soul. In September 1997, Mr. Turnley received a life sentence for his role in a conspiracy to possess and distribute both cocaine and crack cocaine. As the reality of life behind bars set in for Mr. Turnley, his focus suddenly shifted. He vowed that if he ever saw the outside of prison walls, he would trade his life of self-satisfaction to one of servitude. He became a model prisoner and began to "learn other people."

On April 6, 2016, Larry Turnley was resentenced for third time and after serving 19 years in custody, he

was immediately released to five years' supervised release. He was not afforded the opportunity for reentry services, and I was sketchy about what his supervision would look like. Upon our initial meeting, it was apparent that Mr. Turnley was going to be a different sort of intensive supervision case. Within 90 days of his release from prison, he obtained gainful employment, became a certified personal trainer, and established Gladiator X Training, providing free personal training sessions to the public.

Each interaction with Mr. Turnley was noteworthy due to his modest nature. He rarely mentioned his role in community activism and outreach, which were well documented on both social media and throughout the community. Since 2016, Mr. Turnley has co-hosted annual Thanksgiving dinners and coat drives in J.C. Napier and Tony Sudekum Homes, two local housing projects that he resided in as a youth. In 2017, our office donated food items to the dinner, and my family and I served alongside other community volunteers.

During many of our conversations, Mr. Turnley and I often spoke about youth violence, wholistic living, and working towards optimal physical and mental health. He expressed his acknowledgement that he was called to be a community asset and demonstrated his dedication to working to minimize youth deviance and violence. He credits his attitudinal shift to recognizing the importance of following rules and to have an excellent work ethic. His jobs as a sanitation worker in a well-to-do suburb of Nashville, and his night job as a hotel valet at Lowe's Vanderbilt Hotel afforded him opportunities to interact with people of varying races, ages, and socioeconomic statuses. He said working these jobs reframed his thinking, and he formulated a "different aspect of looking at poverty." It also provided motivation and reinforced the importance of financial stability.

On July 18, 2018, Mr. Turnley's motion for early termination of supervised release was granted.

Since his release from supervision, Larry Turnley has dedicated his efforts to working to interrupt youth violence, providing outreach services, and addressing community disparities in Nashville. In

February 2019, Larry Turnley became an Outreach Coordinator for Gideon's Army, a grass roots organization focused on improving the physical, socioeconomic, and social conditions for the North Nashville Community. Also, he volunteers weekly as a physical trainer at the Davidson County, Tennessee, Juvenile Hall. He recently participated in a town hall meeting with 2020 Presidential Candidate Beto O'Rourke.

I recently met with Mr. Turnley and asked him to comment on the strengths and weaknesses of the U.S. Probation Office in relation to his success on supervised release. He thoughtfully responded that the probation officer's support of his community activities helped him establish a sense of trust and comfortability with his officer. He also noted that many offenders operate from paranoia, and the disconnect between the power structure (i.e. – criminal justice system) and citizens and/or persons under supervision is prevalent. He emphasized that supervision officers who demonstrate sincerity and credibility can effectively minimize this phenomenon. He discussed the importance of mentoring, as he stated, "people are a reflection of leadership." Mr. Turnley also emphasized that effective supervision requires a connection between the person under supervision and the officer that focuses on individuality as opposed to the "assembly line process." As I reflected on our conversation, it led me to evaluate my supervision practices and how they affect persons under supervision. I believe that communication and mutual respect are paramount to effective supervision. Also, a balanced supervision approach allows officers to maintain authority yet provide positive reinforcement to persons under supervision is integral to effective community supervision. Larry Turnley's success on supervised release illustrates the importance of collaboration between the person under supervision and the U.S. Probation and Pretrial Services Office in the reentry process.

VISIONARY

I use every situation as a part of my training...

Poem by Author

America here I COME

Fresh out the womb for the past 20yrs I been incubating,

Mind, body, and spirit transformed as I mastered TIME patiently waiting.

The Chapter I been preparing 4 is this moment y'all are witnessing,

LIFE without parole didn't break me; it only prepared me 4 my many victories.

Done SEEN IT ALL but not trippin because it was only motivation,

Corporate America be on notice, I'm on my way wit a lot of drive and determination.

Well, I'm here NOW with a Blueprint to bring about much SUCCESS,

As I start this new journey, GOD continue 2 guide me, because I recognize I'm BLESSED!

I drafted this poem while in prison with the anticipation that my motion, which was in the courts, would be **GRANTED**. I wanted to say it when I walked out the prison gates as my family was recording this life changing moment. However, God and the Ancestors had another plan.

At the age of twenty-four, I was sentenced to Life in federal prison after a two-and-a-half-week trial for Conspiracy and Possession with intent to Distribute Cocaine and Cocaine Base/Crack in 1997. My sentence was reduced to 24yrs in 2009 because of the change in the Crack Law during President George W. Bush's administration. Then in 2016 at the age of 43 I was given an immediate release from federal prison because of another change to the Federal Drug Laws during President Barack Obama's administration, after serving 20 years in federal prison.

Under normal circumstances before a person is released from federal custody, they are given prerelease classes to get assistance with putting a financial plan together, help with employment and living arrangements. The same goes for when a person is released to the Federal Halfway House which 90% of people returning from federal prison go to. These programs play a significant role in ensuring that returning citizens have access to vital resources to aid them for a successful return and a gradual smooth transition back into society. When I got immediately released by the courts in 2016 after being removed from society for twenty years, I was given two hours to get off federal property. The only thing I was asked by my case manager was, how would I prefer to be transported home by bus or did I have family that could get me? My response was what is the fastest way, he said bus, I said get my ticket ready! I did not get an opportunity to participate in any pre-release classes or go to the half-way house because my scheduled release date was not until December 2018.

What many people do not know is that in the Feds when I was incarcerated, to be eligible to take a lot of programs that would be helpful to you when you are released, you must be at least two years close to your release date. The only way people with a release date outside of that range could enroll in a program like that is if no one wanted to take that class. Which hindered a lot of people with lengthy sentences from having access to programs that could help them get a trade in prison. Once I was suddenly released, my focus was trying to build relationships with my three adult children (who were babies when I left) and the rest of my family. After that, getting acclimated to an unfamiliar environment and all this modern technology was my focus. My first contact with money came the day after my release as I was given a tour around Nashville. I was given different sums of money from numerous people as I stopped by various locations to let people see that I was free. It is quite common for people to give you money after getting released from prison. Which also sparks the debate of "Why are people treated better getting out of prison than people going to and getting out of college?" My guess is in our (Black) community we know more people going to prison than going to college. As I mentioned, I received sums of money from various individuals, but my mind was not on saving any of the money. Matter of fact when I got out my mind had shifted back to my old way of thinking and what I mean by that is, me feeling as if I had to be the one to take care of everything. I was conditioned to be the one to pick up the tab when I went out with people. One instance that comes to mind is the second or the third day I was out I was given a coming home party at Dave and Buster's. It was a surprise, so I had no knowledge of who was going to be present. After arriving I was able to meet various individuals who I had not talked to in almost two decades. I also received money from numerous individuals at this gathering. Having money in my pocket made me feel like my old self when I was the Man in the City. So, at the end of the night everybody had finished eating, talking, and waiting on the tab. I am sitting back observing the room trying to see who was going to take care of the tab. Maybe it was my mind playing tricks on me however after not seeing anyone going in their pockets to pay for their food and understanding that it was my surprise party. I asked for the tab and paid for about fifteen people's food two days after being released from doing twenty years. So, like I said, "I diverted back to that old type of thinking prior to going to prison." I had numerous occasions after that where people would take me out to eat and I pay the tab. I was doing that on the regular not even thinking about what was in store for me in future or in the coming months. This went on for about 6 months, until I had a sit down with my cousin and we discussed a situation pertaining to property that I had thought I obtained prior to going to prison. After talking with him and learning that the property was now in his name and if I wanted the property, I had to purchase it from him. My thought processes shifted because the whole time I was incarcerated I was thinking that this property was mine with a plan to rebuild it when I got out. Prior to going to prison I put a down payment on the property which was in my grandmother and my cousin's name. Now after my release from prison and having this conversation, this was the first time that I am aware that the property had been solely placed in my cousin's name and he had taken over the property. His conversation to me that day was, "The property is no longer worth what it was at the time the down payment was placed, it's worth much more. If you want to acquire the property, you will have to give me the current price of what the property is worth today." After this conversation he departed, and I was left to ponder," how am I going to produce the money to purchase this property?" Which has now increased ten times from the original purchase price. It was at that moment that the Idea of wanting to save $100,000 in five years came to life. The reason

I said five years is because I was on five years' probation which to me was equivalent to still being locked up. It was more of a way for me to set a goal while on probation and challenge myself on how much I could save in five years. I figured by saving $100,000 I could offer it to my cousin in hopes that he would release the property to me or be able to buy another house once my probation was completed. After that initial meeting with my cousin, my quest to save $100,000 in five years started. To embrace the challenge, I knew I had to change the way that I was spending. Which called for me to abandon that "you only live once mindset." The best thing that I had going for me was, I did not have a car note and I did not have a house note so I was able to remove those two expenses from my list of monthly payments. The reason I did not have a car note is because I was given a vehicle when I was released, and I chose to make that car last for five years. As to housing, during my incarceration my cousin and mother worked out a deal once she was unable to make payments. He told her if she were alive, she could live in the property rent free which he continued to honor that agreement between her and him after my release. This gave me an opportunity to house hack by staying at the property with my mother rent free, however after my release I did continue to pay the taxes on the house every year just to show appreciation. I started this book off talking briefly about me serving twenty years in federal prison. I never knew how my experience in prison would be so valuable in my quest to save one hundred thousand dollars. But relying on those disciplines and structures I acquired over two decades in prison assisted me mightily. Mainly because it forced me to do more with less and learn to move with a purpose. Everything I did in prison (all the programs I took, classes I taught, situations I overlooked and studying I did) revolved around me obtaining my freedom. Imagine being able to store your whole life, anything of value (food, clothing, legal materials, cosmetics, toiletries, books, jewelry, and money) in a three ft wall locker. Other than being respectful and minding your own business, it does not require a lot of anything to go about your daily activities in prison. You're given three meals, a place to sleep and most federal institutions will provide you with (in most cases) five pairs of pants, five shirts (3 short sleeves, two long sleeves), a pair of boots, five pair socks and five pairs of underwear. This will have to last you your entire stay at the prison. So, if you are at an institution for five, ten, or twenty years that is all you will be allowed to have in your possession according to policy. However, if your clothing becomes worn out from working or exercising in them, you can sometimes do a clothing exchange for some used clothes and boots. But that is up to the laundry department because every eighteen months from the date you arrived at that institution is your clothing exchange date to get a sometimes "new" issue of clothing. Once I shifted my mind to saving, I chose to adopt that concept out here. Having that experience of living off the bare minimum for 20 years allowed me to program my mind on not spending a lot on clothing out here. When I spent money on clothing, I went to goodwill to get used, cheap items. It allowed me to decide in an economical way what style I wanted to create in an inexpensive way. Wearing baggy clothes was the style before I was incarcerated and in prison, now the style is fitted. Goodwill allowed me to find what worked for me for pennies on a dollar as opposed to learning from buying hundred-dollar pants and shirts. During those 20 years in prison, I had become accustomed to wearing used items and making them look new, acceptable, or fashionable. Because it was common for the laundry department to give you used underwear that was clean but still stained from bodily fluids, used socks and boots that had been worn. When people are released from prison or when they go to the hole the Laundry Department will wash, then pass along their clothing to you when you go for an exchange. Which still puzzles me why people get out of prison and spend so much money accumulating excessively name brand clothing and shoes. When most brands sold in prison are cheap and, in most cases, defective. At visit with our loved ones, we made institutional garb look and feel as if we had on Gucci or Saint Laurent. Or we made the sweatsuits and cheap tennis shoes we bought in commissary look and feel as if we had on Polo and Jordan's. In prison we knew it was us that made the clothing what it was. However out here many of us allow material things to define us. I have been out almost six years and to this day 95% of my clothes are hand me downs, used, or gifts and once a year I go buy me a pair of black boots. I buy black boots because they go with everything, I can wear them every day for either working out, for work or going to an event. Saving on housing and clothing was not the only area that I was able to save after being released. I also saved on food using the things I made a habit of eating while in prison. My eating habits changed dramatically when I was in prison. After my third year in prison, I cut out red meat, pork, turkey, chicken from my diet and became a pescatarian. I felt that if I wanted to give myself a chance to outlive my sentence which was Life at the time. I had to start watching what I consumed in my body. I also went a few years as a vegan eating bean, soups/noodles, fruits, vegetables, oats, etc. However, by playing sports in prison my strength was not where it needed to be to play on an elevated level without a high source of protein like fish. So, for about fifteen years of my time in prison I was a pescatarian. To continue my quest to save one hundred thousand dollars I went back to eating like I was in prison. Eighty-five percent of the time I eat noodles, sardines, tuna, boiled eggs, oatmeal, fruits, beans, and vegetables. Which is very inexpensive and cheaper than what things cost in prison. I do not think people really know how expensive it is to do time. The prices are astronomical compared to grocery store chains out here. Imagine going to the store and there is never a sale, a discount and you cannot go anywhere else to spend your money. I learned from my first few months of being free that it's cheaper to shop for your food and cook it than to go out to eat so that is what I started doing. I also learned during that time if you went out anywhere it was going to cost you at least one hundred dollars. Whether that was on gas for your car, food, drinks, or someone asking for money. Knowing this I became a homebody because I preferred that money to go into my pocket. When I got off from work or whenever I finished training a client I went in the house. It did not stop there, here is another concept I referred to when I got out that I used when I was in prison. For most of my time in prison I ran a store selling mostly snacks, coffee and creamer. My goal for my store was to make five dollars a day which was twenty mailing stamps (because mailing stamps was the main bartering tool). That way I could send someone to the store the next day to get five dollars' worth of commissary for me and reinvest back into my store. Some days I made five dollars some days I did not. But that was just a way for me to be content about whatever I made for the day and not get greedy wanting to make more. With my first job being at a Temporary Service agency I knew that it was important for me to apply that same method out here in some kind of way to not get discouraged or distracted because I was starting at the bottom. When I accepted the fact that it was going to be a challenge trying to build a life working at a temporary service agency, several things kept me grounded and focused on my goal. One was me overstanding that, "it's not what you make, it's what you save." Another was working for pennies in prison but creating other opportunities within the job that was more valuable than the money. Like for instance working in the kitchen, although the pay may have been minuscule, being that I was a vegetarian/pescatarian I had access to fruits, vegetables, oatmeal... If I worked in the housing unit I did not have to go outside to work in the cold like other jobs. If I worked on the trash crew, I got an opportunity to come up on anything that was confiscated from other inmates by officers. If I worked on the compound picking up trash, I got the opportunity to move freely without a pass talking to women guards or transporting things for people such as food, laundry, ironed clothes for visit. My work experience in prison gave me a gift in recognizing holistic benefits and not just money. My neighbor who knew me prior to going to prison who I talked to occasionally also kept me focused and grounded. He knew the situation with me and my cousin pertaining to the house. One day a pipe burst in the bathroom, and I was outside in the freezing rain trying to cut the water off from the water meter. He looked out his window and saw me struggling so he joined me. As we got the water shut off to fix the pipe, I guess he heard something in my voice or seen something in my eyes, but it prompted him to say, now mind you he's retired from Nashville Electric Service and living in a million-dollar house next door to me, "Everybody's blessing is their blessing just as your blessing is yours. Don't pay attention to how other people are living yours will come just keep doing what you're doing." I looked at him and said, "You're absolutely right, I prayed to have these problems out here." In my mind I knew that if I applied what I learned from my experiences in prison to every situation I encounter here in society I would be successful. Because when I was in prison, I was in the best shape of my life mentally, physically, and spiritually. All I had to do was move with a purpose and be intentional in manifesting my vision to save one hundred thousand in five years. Prior to seeking employment when I came home, I tried to first start my own personal training business, which was something else I acquired while in prison. I got certified as a personal trainer in prison to teach fitness classes for the Recreation Dept. at any institution I went to and got paid. I do not know how people can work out, train, do landscaping, paint, or cook in the kitchen for years and decades in prison then get out and do not utilize that skill or talent. However, when I came home, I was giving free group exercise services every Saturday to get my name out there and by doing so I was able to get a few clients to pay me to train them. I was charging $15 for an hour session at Centennial Park. Being that I was not making enough to satisfy my probation obligations or my goal of saving one hundred thousand. I started looking for employment. I wanted something with good benefits and an opportunity to move up within the job and give stability

Year 1:

FOLD OR FOCUS

If you are a Hip-Hop fan and paid attention to most of the successful artists from the streets. Most of them don't achieve real wealth until they transform their street mentality.

So, the first job I applied for was working for the City/Metro at the Music City Center in downtown Nashville. The jobs I was applying for was either housekeeping or setting up for events both had good pay and good benefits. Being that my father was already working there for the temporary worker service and was cool with the guy that did the hiring for the Music City Center I was given an interview as soon as I applied. Once I told him about me just getting out of prison and how much time I served. He suggested that I go through the temporary worker service agency for ninety days and after the ninety days he would evaluate my work ethic. If I did well without any issues, he would hire me full time. The Temp Service Agency was not the route I wanted to take when it came to finding a job. I was looking for something more stable like a hospital or warehouse. Then when I found out I would be getting paid nine dollars an hour, the only thing that kept me motivated was getting hired full time in ninety days. I got on with the temp service and made a goal to save one hundred dollars a day. Since I was only making seventy dollars a day with the temp service, and I had a few clients I was training on the side with my personal training. This was a doable and realistic goal. I also had a couple of friends that had their own businesses who I worked part - time for when my training was slow. I chose one hundred dollars because I did not want to start thinking that I needed more money than that to survive out here and set myself up. Because it is easy to get caught up in keeping up with the Joneses and end up back in jail. Since my truck was given to me, and I did not have any rent to pay, three thousand dollars a month was cool with me. Everything was going smoothly at the Music City Center and my arduous work doing housekeeping was getting recognized by all the supervisors I worked for. Because of that the temp service made sure I got all the hours and days I wanted which increased my ability to save more money. Working at the Music City Center had many health benefits because it required me to do a lot of walking as I cleaned all the restrooms and glass windows inside the 2.1 million square ft building. Also being in downtown Nashville made it so therapeutic after being locked up for two decades inside of a fence. Getting the opportunity to hang out on the numerous balconies at the Music City Center at night looking out at the tall buildings, large crowds and bright lights was refreshingly intoxicating to my spirit and mental health. Those ninety days went by in a blur, and I was ready for my evaluation to see if I would be brought on permanently to work for the Music City Center. During those ninety days I had worked with and worked around the individual that was going to determine if I would be hired away from the temp service. Everyone had wonderful things to say about my work ethic including him, however after our meeting it appeared as if my status as a convicted felon played a role in me not getting hired on.

The guy stated that he needed to evaluate me ninety more days because he was not sure how I would react to someone if they made me lose my cool. I just looked at him in disbelief as if this news was not enough to make me lose my cool after working for a low wage around so many difficult characters and personalities for ninety days. I told him thank you and I will continue to work hard in hopes of getting hired on permanently in ninety days. After that meeting I started to explore my options for finding a better paying job which came a few weeks after that meeting. A few weeks after the meeting a friend of mine called and asked if I needed a job, so I explained to him my situation. He was a cook at the Bridgestone Firestone Distribution Center in La Vergne, Tn. A guy that he cooked for asked him if he knew of anyone that could drive a forklift and would like to work for the company he managed, LACOSTA that had a contract there. My friend asked me if I could drive a forklift and if I could, the pay was $11 an hour and I could start as soon as I passed a drug screen. This was another situation where my experience in prison created an opportunity for me. Because during my time in prison I took a forklifting class and got certified to operate a forklift which I took the certificate to the interview with me when I was hired. I notified and informed the temp service agency and my supervisors at the Music City Center that I had found a new job paying more money and I was no longer going to be working for them. Everyone expressed how much they were going to miss me and wished me much success on my new opportunity. My new job with LACOSTA oversaw housekeeping at the Bridgestone plant. We cleaned up spills from the machines that made tires for vehicles, restrooms and we emptied small dumpsters that were placed throughout the inside of the plant with a forklift. We took the dumpsters to an area in our shop and dumped them in a large trash compactor then returned them back to where we got them. However, most times we would take a dumpster with us to replace the dumpster we were taking because we did not want the workers at the plant to not have a place to dispose of their waste. Learning to go up and down on the elevator with those dumpsters was very intimidating at first but I caught on quickly. So quick that after my first month in a half I became a supervisor which came with a pay increase. My goal was to eventually get hired on with Bridgestone to work at the plant making tires. Becoming supervisor was something I was proud of, and it came with a lot of responsibilities because most of the time I was the only worker in the shop during this shift. This new role required me to continue dumping dumpsters however I was also asked to answer all emergency calls throughout the plant. Which consisted of cleaning up major spills if a machine got backed up, whether that was from water, oil, or carbon. The carbon was the hardest and most demanding one to clean because it was powdery. Bridgestone uses carbon to make the tires black by inserting it into a machine that would load it into another machine that manufactured the rubber. But sometimes the carbon would get backed up and spill out into an overflowing area. It was not uncommon to see carbon piled up 2 ft high and in a 7 by 9-foot space. When this happened, I would get a call on my radio to come to the area to clean it up. I put on the personal protective equipment and grabbed the vacuum which was in deplorable condition to suck it up. After doing this a few times I noticed I was still blowing black carbon out of my nostrils two and three weeks after cleaning up the spill. Feeling it was unhealthy and hazardous to my body, I left that job after three months. Although I spent a short amount of time at Bridgestone this job prepared me for unexpected hard demanding work sometimes two three times a day. To this day that was the hardest job I ever had. Even when I was working at Bridgestone on my off days, I was still doing a few training sessions on the side, working with my friend at his cleaning business cleaning up buildings and working with another friend doing pressure washing. So, as I was looking for another job, I was still maintaining my goal of saving one hundred dollars a day. Not long after I left Bridgestone a friend suggested that I check out a company called Red River Waste Solutions. He told me he once worked there, and a friend of mine was currently working there. I called my friend that worked there and asked him about the job, he mentioned that he had been there about eight years and he loved it. After talking with him and the friend that suggested the company, they reached out to the supervisor of the company who scheduled me for an interview. Within weeks of leaving Bridgestone, Red River hired me to work on a trash truck making twelve dollars and fifty cents an hour as a rear loader picking up trash. From my time in prison, I remembered that one of the best jobs to have in there was working on the trash crew. Mainly because of all the things you could come across and have access to. My savings went to another level at this time because the only bills that I had was a phone bill, gas for my car, insurance and I was giving my mother money monthly to take care of all the bills that came to the house along with some of her medical bills. I was able to not only get paid doing the work of the company as a trash collector, but I also now found out that I could get tips on the job. Which reminded me of working in prison and creating multiple benefits or opportunities from one job. I started working at Red River at the end of November 2016, it was around Christmas time. I did not know before this that most customers give their trash collector tips for Christmas to go along with their paycheck. Keep in mind when I say tips from the customers, I mean through the week you may have 500 to 600 stops or pickups. Now just think around Christmas you got five to six hundred stops and each one of those customers give you anywhere between five and one hundred dollars. Getting $5000 in tips picking up trash along with your paycheck was normal during Christmas. Some drivers were said to get up to ten thousand in tips, however they had bigger routes to pick up and did not have to split their money with helpers, which was one of the advantages of having your own route by yourself.

Year 2:

SERENDIPITY

Don't wait till you broke to be CREATIVE. Become CREATIVE when you are getting some money!

I worked as a rear loader and helper for about four months until I got my own route as a Satellite Driver with a dollar and fifty cent pay increase. My job as a Satellite Driver required me to go in people's driveway to their backdoor and get their trash. This service was for the elderly who could not push their trash can out to the street or people that had money to pay for this service. During this time is when I saw how many other different benefits and opportunities were within this job. As I worked as a Satellite driver, I started to see that there were benefits in the things you picked up. Which made the saying, "another person's trash is another person's treasure" ring loud! I retrieved a lot of valuables from the trash during my two plus years of working for Red River. I was picking up in Belle Meade, Brentwood, West Meade, Oakhill, Bordeaux, Bellevue, Donelson, Greenhill's you name it and there was a lot of quality things that people threw away. My co-workers used to make fun of me for going inside the trash bags looking for items, they called me a dumpster diver. However, I did not care because I found some amazing things on my route. For example, I had this guy whose house I serviced. I did not know if his wife had passed or what, but I had seen him on numerous occasions when I picked his trash up and I never saw anyone else but him. On one occasion when I went to pick up his trash, there were a lot of things placed in boxes around the trash can. When I looked in the trash can, I could see it was at its capacity with boxes, which let me know that the items in the boxes outside the trash can were trash too. When I dumped the trash can into my truck, I heard breaking glass which was supposed to be dumped with recycling. That is when I started to inspect the inside of my truck and the boxes on the ground outside my truck. It did not take me long to notice that the noise came from some broken crystal wine and champagne glasses that I dumped inside the truck. I gathered the ones that did not break and placed them inside the boxes on the ground. Then I pulled some of the other boxes out of the truck that was inside the trash can when I dumped it and placed them inside the cab of the truck. To avoid spending too much time in the driveway I threw the rest of the boxes inside the cab of the truck with me. This went on at this stop for about three weeks with boxes placed outside and inside the trash can and I grabbed what was to my liking and discarded the rest. After accessing what I grabbed from that stop It appeared that most of the items had been wedding gifts that were never opened or used, from cookware, gold trimmed champagne glasses, wine glasses, sterling silver serving trays, ceramic dishes, etc. This was not the only spot that I went to that had valuable things, one house in Belle Meade had so many name brand bottles of wine inside the trashcan and outside the trash can that they were getting rid of. Some pickups had clothing and shoes which I kept all these things because it was allowing me to save money and I did not have any type of complex wearing used shoes or clothing if they could fit me or someone I knew. To this day I am still wearing some of the things I found on my route. Those were just a few of the benefits that I benefited from as a trashman. There were also some intangible things I gathered from my route that were more valuable than any item I found. One was being able to use some of the communities I serviced as a vision board. Being up close to many of the beautiful homes in Belle Meade, Oakhill, Greenhill's, and Brentwood opened my mind up to the many possibilities that were within my grasp. Imagine being confined to prison compounds that were smaller than some of the properties I picked trash up at and some of their driveways were longer than some streets. Just being that close to wealth gave me so much inspiration and motivation. Working as a trashman also helped me learn streets, backroads, interstates and how to get around Nashville when I got out. After being away from Nashville for two decades, I was introduced to a whole New City when I returned. Even the Housing Projects I grew up in, JC Napier had gotten a new facelift. Some housing units had been removed and everything looked different but familiar. Red River and Google Maps helped me learn how to move all around Nashville. I also built some great relationships with my customers on my route. It took a minute because I was replacing one of their favorite trashmen who happened to train me, but he left because Red River would not give him a raise. He was a good trainer, and I was a great learner, so I soaked up all his advice and I watched how he worked. After showing them that I was as dependable, reliable, and trustworthy like my trainer. Some of my customers would have chilled water or soda for me on hot days, coffee or cocoa on cold mornings. Along with candy, pastries, and money. Knowing that I may be some of my customers only human interaction, I made sure that when they wanted to have a conversation, I gave them my undivided attention. Even at the expense of making me lose time on my route. Your time management skills could make a difference between getting caught up in rush hour traffic or getting to the dump before it gets overcrowded or, even worse, closed. If the dumpsite were closed, I would have to start my route late the next day because my truck was already at capacity. I would have to dump my truck first thing the next morning before starting my new route. One customer that stands out to me is this white lady in her late eighties or early nineties who lived in Brentwood. She used to come out with her trash when I pulled up, and she would apologize for not having her trash ready. I always assured her that she was all right, and I did not mind waiting for her. Over time, we discussed how much Nashville has grown, our families, her late husband, etc. One day as we were talking, I told her that I was doing a Christmas Coat drive and she volunteered to give me a donation for some coats. Another time we were talking, and I mentioned that my church was doing a yard sale and a fish fry. That's when she told me that her husband had passed, and he had some clothing that she wanted to get rid of. She needed somebody to come remove a lot of his belongings because she was about to move to an assisted living facility. I could tell that she didn't want to go but she knew that she could no longer safely remain in her home. She asked if I could come by to help clean out some of her closets, so one weekend when I was not working, I stopped by in my personal truck to remove the items. I removed everything she suggested for the yard sale. She showed me photos of her in her younger days, wedding pictures of her and her husband. I could tell that this was a special moment for her. She also gave me a Chinchilla fur coat that was like new because the label was still inside the coat. Our conversations on her back porch lasted fifteen to twenty minutes some time, she had a very sharp mind and was highly intelligent. However, before I resigned from the company, I had noticed she had stopped coming out to talk and there was no trash present in her trash can when I made my stop. I do not know what happened to her. Maybe she transitioned to the assisted living facility, but I could tell she enjoyed my company. It was quite common on backdoor stops to experience the passing of customers since most of them were elderly. As I mentioned earlier, my savings went to another level when I started working as a trashman and the opportunities kept coming or should I say I kept recognizing them. One day I heard one of the supervisors talking about a guy they hired to wash the trash trucks. It seemed like he was missing, nowhere to be found, or they couldn't retain him. They needed someone to wash the trucks during the weekend when the trucks were not being used. I was quick on my feet. I called my friend who I was doing part-time work for pressure washing. I told him to give Red River a call to see if he could provide his service pressure washing the trucks. He negotiated a price with them and just like that we started washing the trash trucks for Red River. The first time we washed them it took us all day, from the morning till night fall. However, after I did my research and asked what areas they need us to focus on, we were able to wash 50 to 60 trucks within three to four hours. I hired some of the Drivers from Red River to help where they could wash their truck however, they wanted to. I was able to pay them $175 and I made anywhere from $350 to $400 every other weekend washing trucks. That gig lasted for about eight months until a different supervisor took over. He became upset with us because we would not wash the company trash cans for $5 a trashcan. We asked for ten dollars because it required too much work scraping out all the substances from inside the trash cans. It was really an opportunity for the new supervisor to remove us because he was already looking for a reason. So, he canceled the agreement with us and gave the job to one of his friends. This would be the same supervisor who would be responsible for me resigning when I left Red River. Once the job washing the trucks ended, I got a second job doing Valet parking for Loews Vanderbilt, trying to make up for the money I lost washing the trucks. I only worked two days, Saturday and

Sunday from 11:00 o'clock at night to 7am in the morning. I chose the night shift because I got paid ten dollars an hour and I was the only one working, so I did not have to share my tips with anyone. Valet parking was like a vision board for me too. Getting to drive and see all types of exotic cars was some bucket list stuff. I was able to test and see what cars fit me and drove the best. Also, I learned how to start a lot of cars doing Valet at Loews Vanderbilt. Sometimes I would have a guest waiting for their car for ten minutes as I searched for the ignition or start button, which sometimes ended up with me giving them their keys and walking them around to their car because I was unfamiliar with the latest technology. I had to figure out how to operate some of the new ignition designs and start buttons. Cars were different from what they were when I left the street in 1996. When I got the job doing valet parking, I had been at Red River a year and I was sporadically still doing personnel training on the side which I went up on my prices to $25 an hour session. Between Red River and Lowes Vanderbilt, I was working six days a week Tuesday thru Sunday. This schedule lasted for another year and a half and that is when I resigned from Red River.

Year 3:

FAITH

"Ambitious people make many mistakes, the fearful don't make any."

Why did I leave Red River? I left Red River because I was not paid for a paid time off (PTO) day that I took off for. The secretary at the job overheard me talking to another one of my coworkers, I was telling him that, "I was going to interview for a job during my paid time off." The following week when paychecks came out, I saw that my check was less than it normally was so I at the end of my shift I went and spoke with the supervisor. I asked him "why my check was short" and he said, "you didn't work on that day." I showed him where I had paid time off on that day. That is when he said, "you went looking for another job on that day so therefore we didn't pay you." I asked him if that was in the policy, to which he replied yes. That is when I told him, "I no longer wanted to work for the company, and I resigned. I left Red River at the end of January 2019, I was making $160 a day which does not even include the tips I was getting from my customers as well as the items that I was finding and able to sell. This all went down on a Friday, and I say within a few hours, without knowing where I was going to get a job, I got a phone call from a brother asking me if I wanted to work for this non-profit organization. He explained to me what the organization does and how much money they were paying, all I did was listen in amazement. Here I was, just quit my job and not even five hours had passed, and I got an offer to make a $40,000 salary, more than I was making at my previous job. I told him that I was interested. The next morning, which was Saturday, I met with the leader or the founder of the organization Rasheedat Fetuga and another member of her organization Gideon's Army, a Grassroots Organization for Children. We met in the parking lot of the Northwest YMCA where I was about to speak at a workshop to people on federal probation for my former federal probation officer. They peppered me with questions about who I was, where I was from and could I go into all the communities out North Nashville. The guy that reached out to me the night before had filled them in on the Annual Thanksgiving Dinner in JC Napier and Annual Christmas Coat Drive at Napier School that I was doing in the South Nashville Community. I told them that I was about to go give a speech for my former Federal Probation officer and that they could attend. Satisfied with my answers the founder said she had heard enough and to be looking out for a call from her in the next couple days. They left, and I went on the inside to attend the workshop.

I want to take this moment to speak on the fortuitous relationship I formed with my former Federal Probation Officer. We all know that it is not uncommon for returning citizens to have an adversarial relationship with their probation officer, mine was no different. As time went on, Mrs.Darial Washington-Blackledge recognized my work ethic, community engagement and how I advocated for myself. I was honored to hear her express what she saw in me which led to discussions of me becoming a Federal Probation Officer. Mrs.

Washington-Blackledge discussed this opportunity with me because I was passionate about helping returning citizens transition back into society. Returning citizens need to know that they have someone that can identify and empathize with those released back into society from the special housing unit. There are many situations that a returning citizen goes through that only someone that has been in their position can help address it. Me and Mrs. Washington did not start off agreeing completely, I thought that she was trying to send me back to prison, popping up at my house early in the morning on Sunday's, right before I was to get off from night shift at my Valet job. Mrs. Washington-Blackledge was unpredictable, and I believed she thought I lived at a different address, or she wanted to know if I was really at work because she kept popping up at my jobs. However, after I had a talk with her about how I felt, she explained her intent and after that she became one of my biggest supporters. One year, her office supported my Annual Thanksgiving Dinner in JC Napier, and her children volunteered to serve the food. In 2018 and throughout 2019 Mrs. Washington was diagnosed with cancer and it started to take a toll on her in 2020. After hearing about it I reached out to her and told her if she needs anything to reach out to me, and I felt honored when she did! Mrs. Washington called me and said Mr. Turnley, can you take me to get my treatment. I said of course, she gave me the address, date and time and I picked her up at her house. Seeing that she could not even walk without assistance hit me hard. Because I remember how strong and agile, she once was popping up at my house and job during surprise visits. She informed me that she may doze off because of the meds she was on, she had a slurred speech, but her mind was still there. She kept trying to give me references of people that I could work with on a program she was putting together. After we visited Sarah Cannon Cancer Center for treatment, I took Mrs. Washington's to get a smoothie and drove the long way back from the hospital to her house, letting her listen to the radio. I met her four years ago, and in my mind, I could not believe that she was in this type of condition. I saw Mrs. Washington one more time after that when I returned her quilt to her that was given from the Sarah Cannon Cancer Center. After that she called me and told me to meet her dad at one of her properties to see if he needed any help making some repairs. I met him and we talked briefly. He said he had flown in from California and everything with the property was ok. I gave him my number and left. On February 7, 2021, Mrs. Washington passed away. I got the news from a brother that was also on her caseload that she was trying to help become a part of her program. Mrs. Washington was so amazed by my transition back into society, she even wrote to a national radio show about my success being on supervised release. Mrs. Washington was about to take the head position at the Federal Probation Office before her health took a turn for the worse. I know as human's things are beyond our control. However, understanding this does not stop me from imagining," My personal What If?" I know that I mentioned earlier that the reason I chose "five years" to save one hundred thousand dollars was because that is how much probation I had. However, because of all the things I was doing in the community, maintaining gainful employment, passing all my drug screens, and not getting into any trouble my probation was terminated after twenty-seven months of being out of prison.

Later, that day I was contacted by Gideon's Army and told that I was hired. My job would be with a new program that Gideon's Army was implementing called "Violence Interrupters" because it consisted of stopping or quelling retaliatory gun violence in the streets of North Nashville. Which also called for building relationships with communities, businesses, and political leaders. In 2018-2019 a lot of teens were getting shot and killed in the streets. I was already looking for an opportunity to help save our youth. Gideon's Army Violence Interrupter Program provided me with the time and resources to focus on youth violence and this opportunity was a dream come true. My prison experience made this job effortless because every day in prison you got to talk somebody out of crashing out or doing something reckless. Especially if you were a Leader in prison!! Also, being in the Feds will educate you quickly on political leaders because they have so much power on the laws that affect you. One may not know this, but people studying and passing out copies of U.S. Supreme Court Cases, copies of New Bills being introduced in Congress, or New Laws about to be enacted were common when I was on the inside. For two decades, I watched CNN eight hours a day and Sixty Minutes every Sunday hoping to hear anything about a change in federal drug laws. I never knew how organizing picnics and alliances with brothers in prison would be helpful with organizing cookouts and communities on the streets. Once I got on with Gideon's Army, I resigned from my job at Loews Vanderbilt doing Valet Parking. I was still doing my fitness and personal training sessions with clients in the mornings before I started my workday with Gideon's Army. Our first year as Violence Interrupters contrary to what the naysayers say, we were very instrumental in lowering the crime rate seven or nine percent. This task was only in the 37208-zip code which had the highest incarceration rate in America at the time. According to crimegrade.org, the rate crime in 37208 was 92.10 per 1,000 residents during a standard year. All the other areas in Nashville had an increase in its crime rate that year. As the year went on, I started getting noticed by people in politics for my work in the community. As the 2020 Presidential Campaign started heating up, I had a sit down with then- Democratic Presidential Candidate Beto O'Rourke from Texas. I was later invited to sit on a panel with Time Magazine's Most Influential Desmond Meade from Florida. In 2019 Democratic

Presidential Candidate Kamala Harris and now Vice President tweeted a photo I was on about voter registration here in Tennessee. In that same year I was hired to be Democratic Candidate Tom Steyer's Regional Organizing Director in Dec of 2019.

Year 4:

LAW OF ATTRACTION

"Many waste a lot of time trying something New, instead of focusing their time on what they are already great at!"

I was employed by Tom Steyer to work on his 2020 presidential campaign from January to March, but he suspended his campaign in February. I made about sixteen thousand dollars in three months working for Tom Steyer. However, my experience working for him was priceless! Coming from having Life in federal prison to working as Regional Organizing Director on a Presidential Campaign was monumental for me. I am grateful for Tequila Johnson, the first Black woman in Tennessee to be the Regional Director of a Presidential Campaign. She believed in me and helped me get involved in numerous political opportunities. Working for Tom Steyer was not just a job, I believed in his platform for Criminal Justice Reform and Reparations for African Americans. Tom Steyer was the only candidate that ran his campaign on Reparations. My prison experience was instrumental in getting hired to work on the campaign because of Tom Steyer's platform on Criminal Justice Reform which I used while campaigning for Tom. I remember going to Cumberland

County here in Tennessee to speak at a Democratic event. It was right before the primaries here in Tennessee and all the Democratic candidates sent their organizers to speak for them. The room was crowded and 99% of them were white Democrat voters and I was the only African American speaker. Seeing that this rural area suffered from meth addiction I knew that they were experiencing the same effect that crack had on me and my community. Relying on that and the stories I heard from white guys when I was incarcerated who had Meth cases. Allowed me to speak openly about being in prison for twenty years after being sentenced to Life for selling Crack cocaine, getting out after my sentence was reduced and having a positive effect on my community. After discussing the effects of incarceration on children and parents ,then tying all that into Tom's Criminal Justice platform. At the end of the event, I had so many of the voters and other speakers tell me how much they appreciated my speech. Later, one older white guy walked up to me and told me to give him my hand. Unsure of what he was trying to do when I extended my hand to him, he placed a homemade , papier-mache ring made from a dollar bill around my pinky. It was crafty and designed to ensure that the numeral number "One" was facing up and on top as the crown of the ring and said, "You were number ''One `` tonight". You can find this speech on my YouTube page. Around this time, I had already changed jobs with Gideon's Army from a Violence Interrupter to Reentry Coordinator and my pay was increased to a forty-five thousand dollar a year salary. To help me transition into my new role as Reentry Coordinator for Gideon's Army I used my experience from teaching classes and doing programs in prison as my template. Matter of fact the same curriculum I taught in prison is the same one I used for my Reentry Program, which came from author Napoleon Hill's "Keys to Success: The 17 Principles to Personal Achievement." That book is responsible for most of what I have accomplished today. The same day the Democratic Presidential election for Tennessee was held, Nashville was hit by a powerful tornado in the community where I worked and lived. It destroyed seventy percent of the area. Minutes after the Tornado that hit March 3, 2020, I was in the streets rescuing and informing my team about the damage that was done. I went Live on Facebook during those dramatic moments checking on people that I had built relationships with, making sure they were O.K and helping other people that were instantly affected. From that act and other acts performed by members of Gideon's Army, along with having our presence already established in the part of the community that was highly affected by the tornado. Gideon's Army took charge in leading the Disaster Relief Recovery and was very influential in the organizing efforts to get resources to people affected by the 2020 tornado. It was also through those same efforts that I met Jeff McGruder from Citizens Bank who would eventually help me to purchase my investment property and start several businesses.

Year 5:

ACCOMPLISHMENTS

> *"Taking classes in prison is called programming. However, taking classes in society is called building a resume. "*

By the year 2021 which was my fifth-year home I reached my goal of saving one hundred thousand dollars in the bank. I was eventually approved for a conventional loan for two-hundred and forty thousand dollars. Once I got approved, I reached out to my cousin to see what he would take for the property. After going back and forth he agreed to sell me the property for two hundred and twenty-eight thousand dollars. He wrote up a contract and all I needed was a bank to give me the money. Because the house needed some obvious repairs from neglect, and the 2020 tornado created more damage. Even when I got a bank to overlook the repairs needed, they came back and denied me because I did not have any credit history. Here I am with one hundred thousand dollars in the bank. Gideon's Army had just given me a pay raise and now I'm making a fifty or a fifty-five-thousand-dollar salary. My credit score was 740, the only bills that I had at that time was the cell phone bill, utilities at the house, insurance and paying for gas and groceries. I had five thousand dollars in the stock market from the first two (the six hundred and twelve-hundred dollar) stimulus checks, and I have a credit card with a thirty-five-thousand-dollar limit. All that and I still could not find a bank to help me. After eight months of searching for a bank to help me close on the property, I reached out to Jeff McGruder at Citizens Bank, and they helped me close on the property in one month. Jeff McGruder and Citizens Savings Bank also helped me start a real estate investment company and a junk removal/valet trash pickup business which got me my first client. Jeff paired me with the Tennessee Small Business Development Center to teach me about running a business. After making a fifty-five thousand dollar down payment on the investment property I immediately gained over two-hundred thousand dollars of equity in the investment property. Now because of Citizens Bank, which is one of only twenty black banks in the United States, I will be featured in the February 2022 edition of Independent Banker magazine. In August of 2021 I resigned from Gideon's Army to dedicate my time to my businesses and focus on building my Brand/Legacy. The same way I used my experience from prison to aid me in accumulating one hundred thousand dollars. I'm now going to use my job experiences to help me become financially free. Monetizing and leveraging your skills or gifts is the Blueprint to becoming successful in this new economy. Speaking of which, I have now started getting compensated, although small, to do speaking engagements. I am reminded of something Steve Harvey said, which was if people pay you a dollar for something they will pay you $10, if they pay you $10, they will pay you $100, if they pay you $100, they will pay you $1,000 and we see where he is at now by starting off selling jokes for five dollars. See, just like in prison (which I tell people I am going to do a Life sentence out here) I have been remarkably busy adding more value to myself by programming and taking classes. In 2021 alone I completed Stand Up Nashville Boards & Commissions

Leadership Institute which I am now certified to sit on any Board or Commission in Nashville. I completed North America's Building Trades Unions Apprenticeship Readiness Program in which I am certified to join the local Trade Union to start a career in Trades. I also graduated from Columbia Business School and Resilience Education: Financial Empowerment Program through Columbia University's Justice Through Code which taught me everything I need to know to become financially free. Continuing all those good habits I created in prison is what has put me on a solid path to success out here in society. I know that I spoke a lot about saving one hundred thousand dollars, however the main point I want to get across is that every opportunity I was blessed to receive I ADDED VALUE TO IT!! The example and work ethic I bring to any situation I am a part of is unmatched because of my drive, discipline, and patience. Having a PURPOSE and a VISION will help you avoid wrestling with people over their opinions and help keep your ego in check. I could have easily allowed anger, frustration, bitterness, and vengefulness overcome me because of how I felt towards my cousin, my first job when I was asked to give them another ninety days, my supervisor at Red River for taking my side job washing trucks and not paying me for my paid time off and many other obstacles I've faced. The same way I could have allowed anger, frustration, bitterness, and vengefulness overcome me when I was sentenced to Life in Federal Prison at the age of twenty-four for drugs. When at that time in my life many felt I had nothing to gain for being good and nothing to lose for being ignorant. Looking back, I'm thankful for the mentors I had in prison that helped me navigate that environment avoiding pitfalls and landmines while staying focus and patiently waiting on my blessing to get released. I am also thankful for my mentors out here that are helping me navigate a new world and a new way of life trying to be a good example , while waiting on my blessing to be financially free. I do not care where you find yourself in life, if you're alive you have a chance and the only time you cannot change is in the graveyard!! In the words of President Barack Obama, "Information is the Currency of the Twenty First Century," let your CHANGE make your PRESENT valuable and LEARN to leverage your EXPERIENCES into OPPORTUNITIES.

Facilitating Napoleon Hill's "Keys to Success: The 17 Principles to Personal Achievement " for over a decade in Federal Prison helped me absorb and make a habit of using each principle in my day-to-day walk.

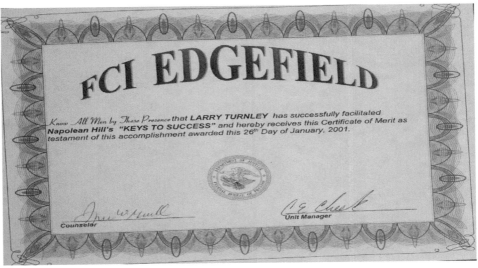

Getting the Training for the "Wake Up" Juvenile Awareness Program opened up opportunities for me to build relationships with the Davidson County Juvenile Detention Center in Nashville, Tn.

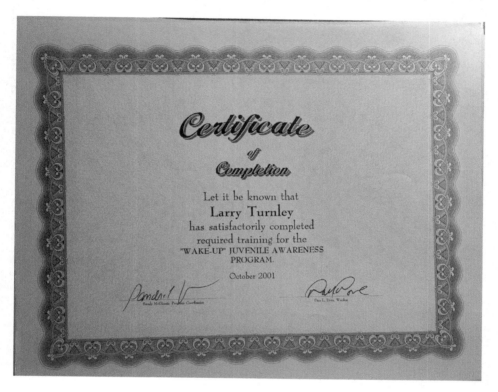

These are a few Photos of me giving every parent of a child at the Davidson County Juvenile Detention Center $100 for Christmas.

Getting this Welding training in prison has added more value to my resume with the Labor Union where I'm currently employed and my The Refuse Engineers Business

These are pictures of the Truck and Trailer to my Towing and Hauling Business.

Me at Tennessee State Small Business Development Center

Fitness Certifications I received in prison that allowed me to teach fitness classes while in prison and helped me start a personal training business when I came home from federal prison.

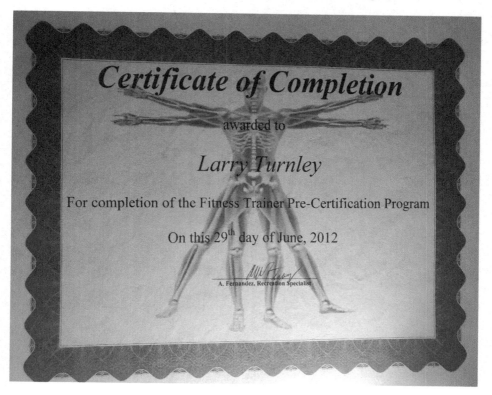

Certificate of Completion

awarded to

Larry Turnley

For completion of the Fitness Trainer Pre-Certification Program

On this 29th day of June, 2012

A. Fernandez, Recreation Specialist

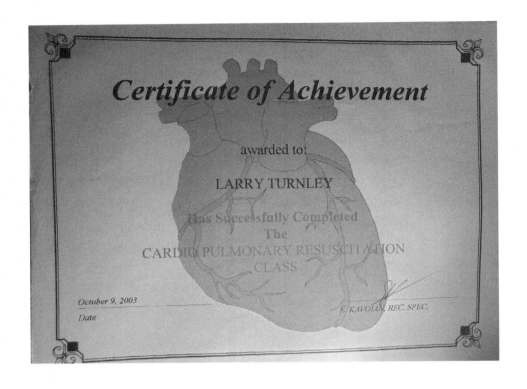

Certificate of Achievement

This certifies that

Larry Turnley

is presented this Certificate of Recognition for

Completion of Sixty Hours in

KINESIOLOGY

from the

Recreation Department

5-19-1999

Date

FCC Beaumont - USP Beaumont
BEAUMONT, TEXAS

Instructor

Supervisor of Recreation

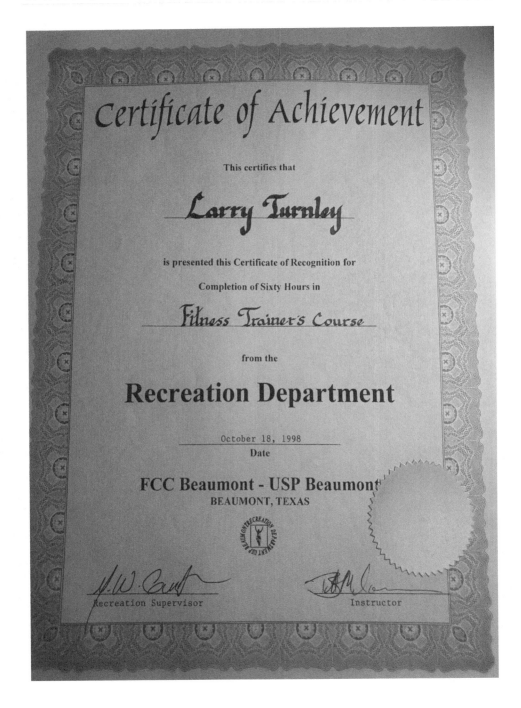

Certificate of Achievement

This certifies that

Larry Turnley

is presented this Certificate of Recognition for

Completion of Sixty Hours in

Fitness Trainer's Course

from the

Recreation Department

October 18, 1998
Date

FCC Beaumont - USP Beaumont
BEAUMONT, TEXAS

Recreation Supervisor   Instructor

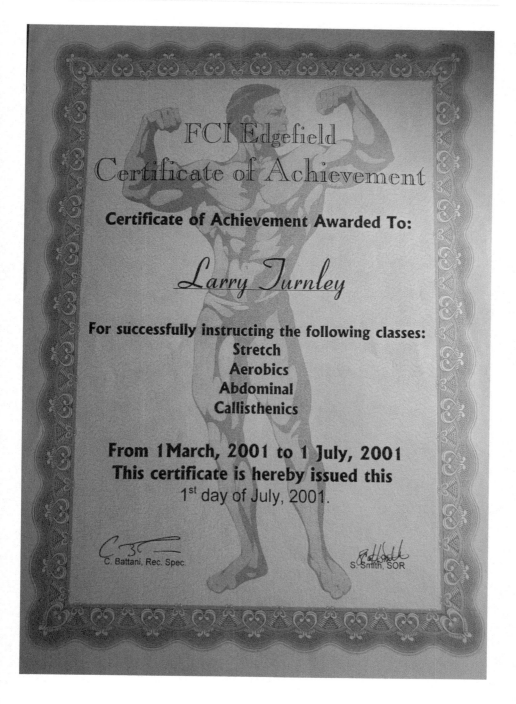

FCI Edgefield
Certificate of Achievement

Certificate of Achievement Awarded To:

Larry Turnley

For successfully instructing the following classes:
Stretch
Aerobics
Abdominal
Callisthenics

From 1 March, 2001 to 1 July, 2001
This certificate is hereby issued this
1st day of July, 2001.

C. Battani, Rec. Spec.

S. Smith, SOR

FCI Three Rivers
Health and Nutrition Class

THIS CERTIFICATE CERTIFIES THAT
Larry Turnley
SUCCESSFULLY COMPLETED
HEALTH AND NUTRITION CLASS
On November 11, 2012

A. Diaz, Recreation Specialist

*FCI Three Rivers
Recreation Department.*

TURNLEY

On this the 17th of June of our Lords year, Two-Thousand and Ten.
You exhibited professionalism, integrity and the ability to
Teach, Abdominal #2 Class.
" GOALS ARE THE FUEL IN THE FURNACE OF ACHIEVEMENT "

F. Aleman, Recreation Specialist

FCI Three Rivers

Here's some pictures from the Free weekend training sessions I provided for the community when I came home from federal prison.

Here's the Forklift Certification I received in federal prison and used to get a job at the Bridgestone plant.

Here the Bank Statement from when I took out $55,000 for the down-payment on my investment property.

BANK OF AMERICA

P.O. Box 15284
Wilmington, DE 19850

BANK OF AMERICA
Preferred Rewards

Customer service information

📱 1.888.888.RWDS (1.888.888.7937)

En Español: 1.800.688.6086

🖥 bankofamerica.com

✉ Bank of America, N.A.
P.O. Box 25118
Tampa, FL 33622-5118

🔔 Please see the **Important Messages - Please Read** section of your statement for important details that could impact you.

Your Bank of America Advantage Savings Preferred Rewards Platinum

for February 24, 2021 to March 26, 2021

LARRY DONNELL TURNLEY JR

Account summary

Beginning balance on February 24, 2021	$76,623.08
Deposits and other additions	3,190.14
Withdrawals and other subtractions	-55,134.20
Service fees	-0.00
Ending balance on March 26, 2021	$24,679.02

*Annual Percentage Yield Earned this statement period: 0.03%.
Interest Paid Year To Date: $3.67.*

Here's my Bank statement balance of $76,623.08

BANK OF AMERICA

P.O. Box 15284
Wilmington, DE 19850

BANK OF AMERICA

Preferred Rewards

Customer service information

  1.888.888.RWDS (1.888.888.7937)

  En Español: 1.800.688.6086

  bankofamerica.com

  Bank of America, N.A.
  P.O. Box 25118
  Tampa, FL 33622-5118

Your Bank of America Advantage Savings Preferred Rewards Gold

for January 27, 2021 to February 23, 2021

LARRY DONNELL TURNLEY JR

Account summary

Beginning balance on January 27, 2021	$75,992.70
Deposits and other additions	3,274.67
Withdrawals and other subtractions	-2,644.29
Service fees	-0.00
Ending balance on February 23, 2021	**$76,623.08**

Annual Percentage Yield Earned this statement period: 0.02%.
Interest Paid Year To Date: $1.99.

Here's my Robinhood Statement Balance of $4,187

Robinhood

■ Options

Portfolio Allocation

Account Summary	Opening Balance	Closing Balance
Brokerage Cash Balance	$0.00	$0.00
Deposit Sweep Balance	$0.15	$0.00
Total Securities	$4,506.44	$4,187.46
Portfolio Value	**$4,506.59**	**$4,187.46**

Income and Expense Summary	This Period	Year to Date
Dividends	$1.46	$1.46
Capital Gains Distributions	$0.00	$0.00
Interest Earned	$0.00	$0.00

Cash and Cash Equivalents 0.00%

Equities 100.00%

Options 0.00%

Here's my Bank Statement at my Credit Union of $21,170. This with my Bank of America and Robinhood Statements total over $100,000 in five years.

STATEMENT OF ACCOUNT

DATE MO/DAY/Y	TYPE OF ACCOUNT / TYPE OF TRANSACTION	ANNUAL PERCENTAGE RATE	FINANCE CHARGE	FEES OR LATE CHARGES	CHANGES TO BALANCE	BALANCE
033121 033121	010 SAVINGS ACCOUNT FEES/CHGS PAPER STATEMENT			2.00	PREVIOUS BALANCE 2.00- NEW BALANCE	21170.56 21168.56 21168.56
	DIVIDEND OF $1.03 WILL BE POSTED TO YOUR ACCT 4-01-21					
033121 033121	020 SHARE SECURED LOAN PAYMENT LOAN PAYMNT		13.58		PREVIOUS BALANCE 142.42- NEW BALANCE	4766.72 4624.30 4624.30
030121	070 CHECKING ACCOUNT VSA TFR 02/27 353726 SQ *ASHLEE SQ *ASHLEE NASHVILLE TN				PREVIOUS BALANCE 19.45	1460.58 1480.03
030821	VSA TFR 03/05 289864 SQ *QUACHE SPEN SQ *QUACHE SPENCER MOUNT JULIET TN				145.88	1625.91
030821	VSA TFR 03/06 360116 SQ *ASHLEE SQ *ASHLEE NASHVILLE TN				19.45	1645.36
030821	VSA TFR 03/08 377932 SQ *ARTIST SQ *ARTIST NASHVILLE TN				72.94	1718.30
030821	POS WD 03/05 217354 CASH APP*MARRIA CASH APP*MARRIAGE M 4153753176 CA				1.00-	1717.30
030821	POS WD 03/05 212970 CASH APP*MASTER CASH APP*MASTER DET 4153753176 CA				25.00-	1692.30
030821	POS WD 03/05 363661 CASH APP*SHAWNT CASH APP*SHAWNTRANI 4153753176 CA				100.00-	1592.30
030821	POS WD 03/07 651217 HIS*HISCOX INC HIS*HISCOX INC 888-202-3007 NY				70.83-	1521.47
030921	VSA TFR 03/09 338374 CASH APP*CASH O CASH APP*CASH OUT SAN FRANCISCO CA				117.59	1639.06
030921	POS WD 03/09 450017 SPRINT *WIRELES SPRINT *WIRELESS 800-639-6111 KS				165.14-	1473.92
031021	POS WD 03/09 210365 CASH APP*MELANE CASH APP*MELANESIA 4153753176 CA				225.00-	1248.92
031021	EFT WD IRS 022821 USATAXPYMT 200146903464957				445.00-	803.92
031521	VSA TFR 03/13 389585 SQ *ASHLEE SQ *ASHLEE NASHVILLE TN				19.45	823.37
031621	VSA TFR 03/16 375365 SQ *SHERRIA HES SQ *SHERRIA HESTER HOPKINSVILLE KY				72.94	896.31
031621	VSA TFR 03/16 358198 CASH APP*CASH O CASH APP*CASH OUT SAN FRANCISCO CA				117.59	1013.9
031721	VSA TFR 03/17 359686 SQ *ARTIST SQ *ARTIST NASHVILLE TN				48.62	1062.
031721	EFT WD PLANET FIT CLUB FEES 2107500445397				20.05-	1042
031921	VSA TFR 03/19 298556 SQ *QUACHE SPEN SQ *QUACHE SPENCER MOUNT JULIET TN				145.88	1188
031921	VSA TFR 03/19 328964 SQ * SQ * NASHVILLE TN				296.61	148
32421	VSA TFR 03/24 132793 SQ *ARTIST SQ *ARTIST NASHVILLE TN				48.62	15
32421	EFT WD LIBERTY MUTUAL A0S25848662670				270.70-	12
					5.00-	1

Photos from when I was in the Feds.

Here I was at USP Edgefield 2000-2002 before it was turned back into a FCI.

Here I'm at USP Beaumont 1997-1999

Here I'm at FCI Talladega Alabama 2014-2016 where I was released from federal custody. We were making a political statement for the death of Michael Brown on this photo. "Hands up Don't Shoot"

Here I was at FCI Three Rivers Tx 2010-2014.

In these photos I was at FCI MEMPHIS 2002-2009. I cut my hair off when I went back to court to get my sentence reduced for the change in the Crack Law.

I'm at FCI Three Rivers Tx right here.

At my Valet job Christmas Party at Loews Vanderbilt Hotel

On panel with Time Magazine's Most Influential Desmond Meade speaking about Criminal Justice Reform

At meeting with then 2020 Democratic Presidential Candidate Beto O'Rourke

At our Germantown Campaign office in Nashville, TN

2020 Democratic Presidential election Watch Party

A photo of me in the corner on then 2020 Democratic Presidential Candidate Kamala Harris Twitter Account

At the Women's Rally in Rutherford County

This is Team Tom, we were Tom Steyer's 2020 Democratic Presidential team in the State of Tennessee

At a luncheon supporting Democratic Presidential Candidate Tom Steyer in 2020.

At an event at Hartman Park Campaigning for Democratic Presidential Candidate Steyer in 2020.

At the National Urban League having a panel discussion about Criminal Justice Reform in 2020.

At the Lab in Nashville,Tn having a panel discussion on voter rights restoration 2019.

Getting my Certificate for Graduating the BCLI (Boards and Commission Leadership Institute) Program in 2021

Me at the City Council meeting in 2021 with Gideon's Army asking for $1 million dollars and got it.

Me at the Metro Police Department North Nashville Precinct with Gideon's Army speaking at a community meeting 2021.

My acceptance into STAND UP Nashville's inaugural BCLI program in 2021

Me on a flyer for the YWCA promoting a Panel Discussion on Public Safety in 2020.

Flyer of a panel discussion I was on for voter rights registration.

(L) Min. Ishmael Muhammad takes a moment with Mr. Larry Turnley, who was formerly incarcerated and is now the Outreach Violence Coordinator for Gideon's Army. (R) Prison Reform Student Minister Eric Muhammad presents Min. Ishmael with an award of appreciation.

Me in the Final Call Newspaper at the 3rd Annual Prison Reform Gala in 2019.

Me Speaking at the Tennessee State Department to the Two Generational Grant holders in 2019.

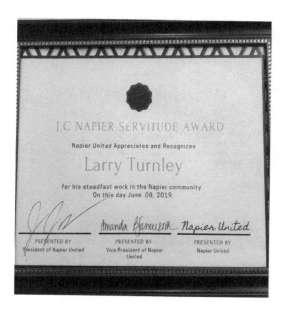

Here's an Award I received for my work in the community in2019

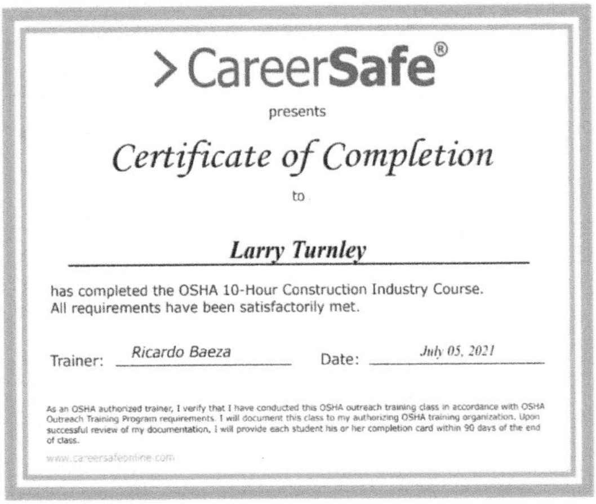

> CareerSafe®

presents

Certificate of Completion

to

Larry Turnley

has completed the OSHA 10-Hour Construction Industry Course.
All requirements have been satisfactorily met.

Trainer: _Ricardo Baeza_   Date: _July 05, 2021_

As an OSHA authorized trainer, I verify that I have conducted this OSHA outreach training class in accordance with OSHA Outreach Training Program requirements. I will document this class to my authorizing OSHA training organization. Upon successful review of my documentation, I will provide each student his or her completion card within 90 days of the end of class.

www.careersafeonline.com

Here's a 10 hr. OSHA certification I got in 2021.

Here is my Certification to sit on any Board or Commission in Nashville.

Here is my Certificate for Graduating the Pre-Apprenticeship Readiness Program for the Trade Union in Nov. 2021.

Here's my Certificate for Graduating Columbia Business School Financial Empowerment Program in Dec. 2021

Here's some pictures from the Annual Thanksgiving Day Dinner in JC Napier and Annual Christmas Coat Drive at Napier School that I started with my childhood friend and Hell's Kitchen alumni Mr.100 Sterling Wright.

Cards and checks receipts from my trash route.

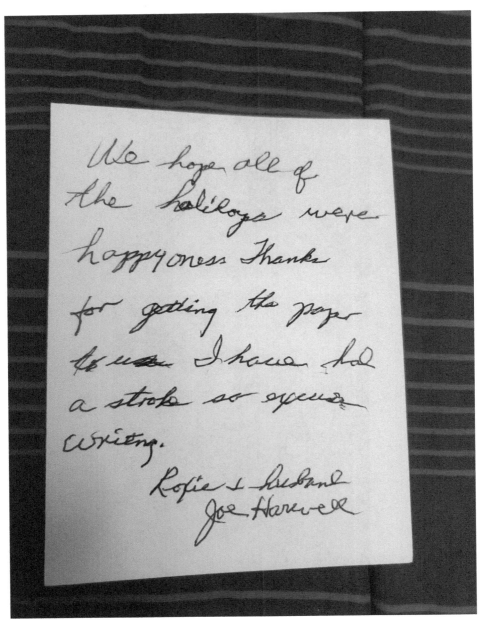

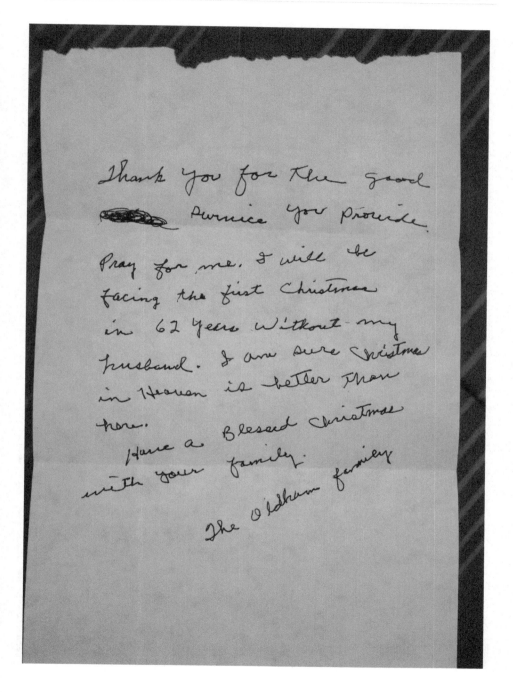

Thank you for the good ~~service~~ service you provide.

Pray for me. I will be facing the first Christmas in 62 years without my husband. I am sure Christmas in Heaven is better than here.

Have a Blessed Christmas with your family.

The Oldham family

Thank you so much for your years of service. I really appreciate all your hard work à picking up my trash at the Backdoor. Especially since I have to use the bungee cords since I have a family of raccoons!

Hope you & your family have a very Merry Christmas!! Susan Hall

Wishing you merry moments, sweet surprises,
and little things that make you smile —
all through the holidays
and through the new year, too!

Susan
6737 Currywood Dr
Nashville, TN 37205

> "AND LO, THE STAR WHICH THEY SAW IN THE EAST
> WENT BEFORE THEM,
> TILL IT CAME AND STOOD OVER WHERE THE YOUNG CHILD WAS."
> MATTHEW 2:9

Xmas 2017

Dear Larry and Family

May all the people of the world
hear and live the message of Christ.
And may His words
bring the peace for which the world is longing.

Christmas PEACE, LOVE and JOY
to you and your loved ones.

May God bless you and your family this
Christmas and throughout the New Year.
Thanks for all of your hard work and taking
extra trash bags and some around the
trash can because they are too heavy for
me to lift.
Diane Bauer

Larry Turnley is a native of Nashville, TN, he is the owner of The Refuse Engineers, he was also the Reentry Coordinator for Gideon's Army. The founder of the J.C Napier Thanksgiving Day Dinner and Napier School Christmas Coat Drive. Larry also was the Regional Organizer for Tom Steyers 2020 Presidential Campaign.

An activist, advocate, business owner, community organizer, credible messenger, innovator, mentor, and returning citizen. He also works at the intersection of public policy & social justice & is actively engaged with local, community-based coalitions & statewide national organizations. Including but not limited; Labor Union; Mayors Police Policy Commission; Metro Nashville Community Oversight Board; NASHVILLE UNCHAINED; NAACP-Nashville Branch; Still Standing; STAND UP! Nashville Boards & Commissions Leadership Institute; The Equity Alliance.

Made in the USA
Columbia, SC
12 May 2022

60089394R00063